Problems of Knowledge and Freedom

Problems of Knowledge and Freedom

THE RUSSELL LECTURES

— BY —

NOAM CHOMSKY

VINTAGE BOOKS

A Division of Random House, New York

The two lectures included in this book were originally published, in slightly different form, in the *Cambridge Review*,
Cambridge, England, in 1971.

Library of Congress Cataloging in Publication Data

Chomsky, Noam.
    Problems of knowledge and freedom.

    (The Russell lectures)
    "The two lectures included in this book were
originally published, in slightly different form, in the
Cambridge review, Cambridge, England, in 1971."
    1. Languages—Philosophy. 2. Knowledge, Theory of.
3. World politics. I. Title. II. Series.
[P106.C53 1972]   121   72-763
ISBN 0-394-71815-1

Contents

— *Introduction* —

THE TASK OF a liberal education, Bertrand Russell once wrote, is "to give a sense of the value of things other than domination, to help to create wise citizens of a free community, and through the combination of citizenship with liberty in individual creativeness to enable men to give to human life that splendor which some few have shown that it can achieve."[1] Among those few who have shown, in this century, the splendor that human life can achieve in individual creativeness and the struggle for liberty, Bertrand Russell holds a place of honor. In reflecting on his life and achievement, the temptation to quote Russell's own words is quite irresistible.

> Those whose lives are fruitful to themselves, to their friends, or to the world are inspired by hope and sustained by joy: they see in imagination the things that might be and the way in which they are to be brought into existence. In their private rela-

[1] *Power: A New Social Analysis* (New York: W. W. Norton & Company, 1938), p. 305.

tions they are not pre-occupied with anxiety lest they should lose such affection and respect as they receive: they are engaged in giving affection and respect freely, and the reward comes of itself without their seeking. In their work they are not haunted by jealousy of competitors, but are concerned with the actual matter that has to be done. In politics, they do not spend time and passion defending unjust privileges of their class or nation, but they aim at making the world as a whole happier, less cruel, less full of conflict between rival greeds, and more full of human beings whose growth has not been dwarfed and stunted by oppression.[2]

When this description of how life should be lived was written, Russell had already changed the course of modern thought with his monumental contributions to philosophy and logic, and was facing obloquy and imprisonment for his determined opposition to a war that he could not accept as just or necessary. Still to come was half a century of creative achievement, not only in thought and inquiry but in an unending, unyielding effort to make the world happier and less cruel. While Russell's intellectual achievements remain a delight to the inquiring mind, it is what Erich Fromm perceptively calls his renewal of the "Promethean function in his own life"[3] that will continue to inspire those who hope to be citizens of a free community.

[2] Bertrand Russell, *Proposed Roads to Freedom—Anarchy, Socialism and Syndicalism* (New York: Henry Holt & Co., 1919), pp. 186–87.

[3] "Prophets and Priests," in A. J. Ayer et al., *Bertrand Russell: Philosopher of the Century,* ed. Ralph Schoenman (Boston: Little Brown and Company, 1968), p. 72.

I need not review here the harassment, the ridicule and abuse that Russell endured in the course of these efforts, the shameful suppression and distortion, the revilement by apologists for the criminal violence of the state. One can only hope that this was more than compensated by the deep respect of decent people throughout the world. I will mention only two small examples. A friend, a young Asian scholar, visiting a tiny island near Okinawa a few months ago, stopped at the home of a farmer who has become the leader of a struggle to free their land from military domination—the movement a curious blend of Christianity and traditional beliefs with a strong populist strain. On a wall, he noticed a poster in Japanese which read: "Which road is the correct one, which is just? Is it the way of Confucius, of the Buddha, of Jesus Christ, Gandhi, Bertrand Russell? Or is it the way of Alexander the Great, Genghis Khan, Hitler, Mussolini, Napoleon, Tojo, President Johnson?"

A second case: Heinz Brandt, on his release from an East German prison, went to visit Russell, whose protest, including the return of a peace medal awarded by the German Democratic Republic, led to his release. As he left, Brandt writes, Russell stood at the door "looking very lonely, very old, [waving] to us with a moving, infinitely human gesture."[4] While Brandt has a more personal reason than most to be thankful for Russell's humanity, his gratitude can be shared by all of those who value reason, liberty, and justice, who are captivated by Russell's vision of "the world that we must seek,"

[4] Heinz Brandt, *The Search for a Third Way* (Garden City, N.Y.: Doubleday & Company, 1970), p. 305.

a world in which the creative spirit is alive, in which life is an adventure full of joy and hope, based rather upon the impulse to construct than upon the desire to retain what we possess or to seize what is possessed by others. It must be a world in which affection has free play, in which love is purged of the instinct for domination, in which cruelty and envy have been dispelled by happiness and the unfettered development of all the instincts that build up life and fill it with mental delights.[5]

Russell sought not only to interpret the world but also to change it. I imagine that he would have agreed with Marx's admonition that to change the world is "the real task." I would not presume to assess or even to try to record his achievement in interpreting or changing the world. To several generations, mine among them, Russell has been an inspiring figure, in the problems he posed and the causes he championed, in his insights as well as what is left unfinished. In these lectures, I will consider a few of the problems to which Russell addressed himself in his efforts to interpret and change the world. The selection of topics reflects my personal interests; others might choose, with equal justice, to emphasize different aspects of his work. I will consider primarily Russell's final summation, in his work of the 1940s, of his many years of inquiry into problems of knowledge, and his social and political thought—expressed in action as well —at about the time of World War I and in the last years of his life.

Is there a common thread running through Russell's enormously varied studies, which, taken as a whole,

[5] *Proposed Roads to Freedom*, p. 212.

touch on virtually every question of vital human concern? Is there, in particular, a link between his philosophical and political convictions? It is by no means obvious that a given person's efforts, in such separate domains, must derive from a common source or be at all tightly linked. Perhaps, nevertheless, one can discern some common elements in Russell's endeavor to discover the conditions of human knowledge and the conditions of human freedom. One point of contact I will discuss briefly in the final paragraphs of the first lecture and the beginning section of the second: the "humanistic conception" of man's intrinsic nature and creative potential that Russell formulates, as he places himself in a tradition of great richness and undiminished promise.

Publisher's Note

The following are the first Russell Lectures, originally presented by Noam Chomsky at Trinity College, Cambridge, in early 1971. The lectures have been slightly revised for presentation in this book.

Problems of Knowledge and Freedom

— 1 —

On Interpreting the World

A CENTRAL PROBLEM of interpreting the world is determining how, in fact, human beings proceed to do so. It is the study of the interaction between a particular, biologically given, complex system—the human mind—and the physical and social world. In the work in which he summarizes a lifetime of concern with this problem, Bertrand Russell asks "how comes it that human beings, whose contacts with the world are brief and personal and limited, are nevertheless able to know as much as they do know?"[1] Studying the relation between individual experience and the general body of knowledge, commonsense and scientific, Russell explores the limits of empiricism and tries to determine how it is possible to attain human knowledge; in particular, he attempts to discover the principles of nondemonstrative inference that justify scientific inference, "in addition to induction if not in place of it." He concludes that "part of empiricist theory

[1] *Human Knowledge: Its Scope and Limits* (New York: Simon & Schuster, 1948), p. v.

appears to be true without any qualification," namely, that "words which I can understand derive their meaning from my experience . . . [with] . . . no need to admit any exceptions whatever." Another part, he concludes, is untenable. We need certain principles of inference that "cannot be logically deduced from facts of experience. Either, therefore, we know something independently of experience, or science is moonshine." His investigation of prescientific knowledge, the knowledge that precedes systematic reflection on the principles of inference, leads to a similar result. His conclusions nevertheless retain "what we may call an empiricist 'flavour' ": though our knowledge of the underlying principles, "in so far as we do know them, cannot be based upon experience," nevertheless "all their verifiable consequences are such as experience will confirm."[2]

We might add that careful efforts to develop an empiricist theory of common-sense or scientific knowledge have generally led to somewhat similar conclusions. For example, David Hume concludes:

> But though animals learn many parts of their knowledge from observation, there are also many parts of it, which they derive from the original hand of nature; which much exceed the share of capacity they possess on ordinary occasions; and in which they improve, little or nothing, by the longest practice and experience. These we denominate Instincts, and are so apt to admire as something very extraordinary, and inexplicable by all the disquisitions of human understanding. But our wonder will, perhaps, cease or diminish, when we consider, that the experimental reasoning itself, which we

[2] *Ibid.,* pp. 522, 524, 526–27.

possess in common with beasts, and on which the whole conduct of life depends, is nothing but a species of instinct or mechanical power, that acts in us unknown to ourselves; and in its chief operations, is not directed by any such relations or comparisons of ideas, as are the proper objects of our intellectual faculties. Though the instinct be different, yet still it is an instinct, which teaches a man to avoid the fire; as much as that, which teaches a bird, with such exactness, the art of incubation, and the whole economy and order of its nursery.[3]

More recent efforts to develop an empiricist theory of acquisition of knowledge also reach conclusions not unlike Russell's. Thus Willard V. O. Quine, though he begins with concepts that seem very narrow and restricted, concludes finally that the innate system of properties (the "quality space") that underlies induction may have an abstract character, and that there are, furthermore, "as yet unknown innate structures, additional to mere quality space, that are needed in language-learning [and, presumably, other forms of learning as well] . . . to get the child over this great hump that lies beyond ostension, or induction."[4] When Quine adds further that by "behaviorism" he refers only to "the insistence upon couching all criteria in observation terms" and eventually making sense of all conjectures

[3] *An Enquiry Concerning Human Understanding,* in David Hume, *Enquiries Concerning the Human Understanding and Concerning the Principles of Morals,* ed. L. A. Selby-Bigge, 2nd ed. (Oxford: Clarendon Press, 1902), p. 108.
[4] "Linguistics and Philosophy," in Sidney Hook, ed., *Language and Philosophy* (New York: New York University Press, 1969), p. 97. Interpolation mine.

"in terms of external observation," he not only abandons behaviorism as a substantive doctrine but also approaches Russell's conclusion that what can be retained of empiricism is only the condition that the verifiable consequences of the principles that constitute our knowledge "are such as experience will confirm."

Perhaps the most austere contemporary representative of the empiricist tradition is Nelson Goodman. In his very important analysis of inductive inference, he shows that the traditional empiricist approach left unresolved "the problem of differentiating between the regularities that do and those that do not . . . set the mind in motion," and suggests that we "regard the mind as in motion from the start, striking out with spontaneous predictions in dozens of directions, and gradually rectifying and channeling its predictive processes."[5] Like Hume, he appeals

> to past recurrences, but to recurrences in the explicit use of terms as well as to recurrent features of what is observed. Somewhat like Kant, we are saying that inductive validity depends not only upon what is presented but also upon how it is organized; but the organization we point to is effected by the use of language and is not attributed to anything inevitable or immutable in the nature of human cognition.

[5] Nelson Goodman, *Fact, Fiction and Forecast* (Cambridge, Mass.: Harvard University Press, 1955), pp. 89–90. Goodman adds that "we are not concerned with describing how the mind works but rather with describing or defining the distinction it makes between valid and invalid projections," but he occasionally discusses the "genetic problem" as well.

The "roots of inductive validity," he suggests, "are to be found in our use of language."[6]

But I think that Goodman rejects too quickly the objection that he is "trusting too blindly to a capricious Fate to see to it that just the right predicates get themselves comfortably entrenched," in the case of the "genetic problem." It is much too facile merely to say that "in the case of our main stock of well-worn predicates, I submit that the judgment of projectibility has derived from the habitual projection, rather than the habitual projection from the judgment of projectibility."[7] This suggestion fails entirely to explain the uniformities among individuals (or across species, even putting aside the problem of explaining induction in the absence of the explicit use of language). If the mind were, literally, to strike out at random from the start, there would be no reason to expect more than fortuitous similarities in judgment, even within the limited range of common-sense predicates that Goodman considers—terms denoting color, for example. In fact, Goodman seems to accept this consequence. Thus he seems to believe that whereas some speakers of English use the word "green" in the way that I assume everyone in the audience does, there are others who mean by "green" what we would mean by the (to us) complex predicate: examined before time t and green or examined after t and blue[8]

[6] *Ibid.*, pp. 96, 117.
[7] *Ibid.*, pp. 97–98.
[8] Cf. Nelson Goodman, "The Emperor's New Ideas," in Hook, ed., *Language and Philosophy*, p. 140: "I am sure that speakers accustomed to projecting 'grue' rather than 'green' would be equally confident that animals use grue rather than green as a basis for generalization."

where *t*, say, might be midnight tonight. These unfortunates will be surprised, tomorrow, to discover that the things they look at and call "green" will match in color some of the things they examined yesterday and called "blue."[9] Goodman's conclusion has the merit of consistency. An austere empiricist, who believes that the mind is in motion from the start, striking out with spontaneous predictions without constraints, should reach this conclusion, along with many others that are equally bizarre. Goodman's analysis directly supports Russell's observation that either we know something independently of experience, or science is moonshine—as are the beliefs of common sense. His further speculations on how, given a system of hypotheses, one might proceed to adduce others, though interesting and suggestive, seem to me to leave quite untouched the central problems of acquisition of knowledge. It seems clear that if empiricism is to be taken seriously, it must be the "externalized empiricism" of Quine which "sees nothing uncongenial in the appeal to innate dispositions to overt behavior, innate readiness for language-learning," and requires only that "conjectures or conclusions . . . eventually be made sense of in terms of external observation."[10]

Recall that in his critique of Locke's *Essay Concerning Human Understanding,* Leibniz conjectured that by admitting reflection as a source of knowledge, Locke leaves the way open to reconstructing a rationalist theory in another terminology. Similarly, one might ask

[9] For a non-question-begging formulation, see my contribution to the same volume, pp. 71–72.

[10] "Linguistics and Philosophy," pp. 97–98.

to what extent even the "flavor" of empiricism is retained in a theory of acquisition of knowledge that
admits a quality space of unknown character, innate
structures of an arbitrary sort that permit the leap to
perhaps quite abstract hypotheses, principles of nondemonstrative inference that Leibniz might have called
the innate general principles that "enter into our
thoughts, of which they form the soul and the connection," principles that "can be discovered in us by dint
of attention, for which the senses furnish occasions, and
successful experience serves to confirm reason."

One might, in fact, reasonably go still further in
chipping away at traditional concepts of acquisition of
knowledge. Why should we suppose that the innate general principles, or the principles that integrate and
organize our mature systems of belief, should be dis-
coverable "by dint of attention"? It would seem to be
an empirical issue whether this is so (apart from ter-
minological debate about the concepts of "knowledge"
and "belief," debate that is likely to be fruitless, since
—as Russell observes—the concepts are unclear and
indeterminate). It is an open question, surely, whether
the "species of instinct" that determines "the experimental reasoning itself" does indeed "act in us unknown
to ourselves," as both Hume and Leibniz held, or perhaps even lies beyond introspection. It is, in fact, possible that insight into or understanding of these matters
lies beyond the scope of conscious human knowledge.
No contradiction follows from assuming this to be so,
though we may hope that it is not. The same innate
principles of mind that make possible the acquisition of
knowledge and systems of belief might also impose

limits on scientific understanding that exclude scientific knowledge of how knowledge and belief are acquired or used, though such understanding might be attainable by an organism differently or more richly endowed. It might be, in Kant's phrase, that the "schematism of our understanding, in its application to appearances and their mere form, is an art concealed in the depths of the human soul, whose real modes of activity nature is hardly likely ever to allow us to discover, and to have open to our gaze."[11] There is, surely, no reason for dogmatic assumptions on this score.

The notion that there may be innate principles of mind that on the one hand make possible the acquisition of knowledge and belief, and on the other, determine and limit its scope, suggests nothing that should surprise a biologist, so far as I can see. Writing on the specific case of postulated innate principles of language structure characteristic of the species, Jacques Monod observes:

> This conception has scandalized certain philosophers or anthropologists who see in it a return to Cartesian metaphysics. But if we accept its implicit biological content, this conception does not shock me at all.

It is quite reasonable to suppose that specific principles of language structure are a biological given, at the present stage of human evolution. Furthermore, Monod continues, it is likely that the evolution of human cortical structures was influenced by the early acquisition of

---

[11] Immanuel Kant, *A Critique of Pure Reason,* trans. Norman Kemp (New York: Random House, Modern Library, 1958), pp. 110–11.

a linguistic capacity, so that articulated language "not only has permitted the evolution of culture, but has contributed in a decisive fashion to the *physical* evolution of man"; and there is no paradox in supposing that "the linguistic capacity that reveals itself in the course of the epigenetic development of the brain is now a part of 'human nature,' " itself intimately associated with other aspects of cognitive function which may in fact have evolved in a specific way by virtue of the early use of articulated language.[12]

Having gone this far, one might well ask whether the residue of traditional empiricist speculation on the origin and growth of knowledge is not more of a hindrance than a help to a successful study of this problem. Consider, for example, the matter of "ostensive definition," which Russell, along with many others, takes to be a primitive or somehow basic stage in the acquisition of knowledge. A vocal noise, it is assumed, is associated with some notable feature of the environment and with an "idea" or "thought" of this feature. The word then "means" this feature in the sense that "its utterance can be caused by the feature in question, and the hearing of it can cause the 'idea' of this feature. This is the simplest kind of 'meaning,' out of which other kinds are developed." It is by reflection on such associations and similarities of stimuli "that the child, now become a philosopher, concludes that there is one word, 'mother,' and one person, Mother." "In time, by the use of Mill's canons, the infant, if he survives, will learn to speak correctly," identifying properly the relevant features of

[12] Jacques Monod, *Le Hasard et la nécessité* (Paris: Éditions du Seuil, 1970), pp. 150–51.

the environment and of the vocal expressions. It is such a process, Russell argues, that in theory leads to the belief in more or less permanent persons and things, the common-sense belief that makes so difficult any philosophy which dispenses with the notion of substance.[13] (Russell adds that he believes "this first step in philosophy to be mistaken," but that is another matter.) Quine suggests a somewhat similar process. For the infant, "mother, red, and water are . . . all of a type; each is just a history of sporadic encounter, a scattered portion of what goes on." The child "has mastered the scheme of enduring and recurring physical objects" only when he "has mastered the divided reference of general terms." After this he reassesses "Mama," retroactively, as a singular term, "the name of a broad and recurrent but withal individual object."[14]

The credibility of such speculations seems to me low, in the light of the little that is known. There is no reason at all to believe that the child's concept of enduring and recurring physical objects derives from his reflection on the use of language or on higher-level generalizations that are built on insights into language use, or that Mill's canons have anything to do with the interpretation of the world of experience in terms of permanent persons and things. Such slight experimental work as exists on this matter suggests that the concept of permanent and enduring objects is operative long before the use of language. Thus it appears that a child

[13] *Human Knowledge*, pp. 75–76.
[14] Willard V. O. Quine, *Word and Object* (Cambridge, Mass.: The M.I.T. Press, 1960), pp. 92–95.

only a few months old interprets the world in terms of perceptual constancies, and shows surprise if stimuli do not manifest the expected behavior of "enduring and recurring physical objects." If our conjectures are to be made sense of in terms of observation, it would seem that such observations support the conjecture that the "scheme of enduring and recurring individual objects" is primitive, rather than acquired in the course of language learning.

Much the same is true when we consider stimuli and their associated "ideas." Surveying some recent experimental work, Monod remarks that there can be no doubt that animals are capable of classifying objects and relations according to abstract categories, specifically geometric categories such as "triangle" and "circle"; to some extent experimental work has even identified the neural basis for such analysis. This work suggests that there is a primitive, neurologically given analytic system which may degenerate if not stimulated at an appropriate critical period, but which otherwise provides a specific interpretation of experience, varying with the organism to some extent. I think Monod is correct in commenting that "these modern discoveries thus give support, in a new sense, to Descartes and Kant, contrary to the radical empiricism that has dominated science for two centuries, throwing suspicion on any hypothesis that postulates the 'innateness' of forms of knowledge." So far as we know, animals learn according to a genetically determined program. There is no reason to doubt that this is also true of "the fundamental categories of human knowledge, and perhaps also other aspects of

human behavior, less fundamental, but of great significance for the individual and society."[15] In particular,
this may be true of man's apparently unique linguistic
faculties, and of his abilities of imaginative thought, as
manifested in language, in visual imagery, in plans of
action, or in true artistic or scientific creation.

A further residue of empiricist speculation appears
in Russell's analysis of proper names. He suggests, to
begin with, that "a proper name is a word designating
any continuous portion of space-time which sufficiently
interests us,"[16] but then adds that spatiotemporal continuity is not required. Again, it is an empirical problem
to determine what are the criteria for "nameability," not
by an arbitrary organism, or what Russell sometimes
calls a "logical saint," but by a biologically given human
mind. Spatiotemporal continuity is no doubt a factor, as
are certain figure-ground and other gestalt properties,
or the function of an object in a space of human action.
But the matter seems still more complex. For example, if
some physical arrangement of objects is created by an
artist as an example of a particular art form, it is nameable—say, a mobile, which need not meet the condition
of spatial continuity. But an arbitrary chance arrangement would not be considered a nameable "thing." If
this is correct, then our concept of "nameable thing"
involves a consideration of the intentions of the person
who produced the "thing." Further analysis would, no
doubt, show other, equally abstract conditions that
underlie the process of naming. It is difficult to imagine
that such conditions are learned, by Mill's canons or any

[15] Monod, *Le Hasard et la nécessité,* pp. 167–68.
[16] *Human Knowledge,* p. 89.

other scheme, though experience no doubt plays some role in refining the innately given schematism for interpretation of the world of human experience. The extent of its contribution is a matter to be determined by scientific investigation. But in this connection too, we should not be surprised if there is some truth to the dictum of the Cambridge Platonist Henry More that "the Soul sings out the whole Song upon the first hint, as knowing it very well before."

It has sometimes been argued that naming is ultimately inexplicable, and that the desire to explain naming beyond recording the facts of usage or providing "tests of the good construction of a series" is "the result of the Protean metaphysical urge to transcend language."[17] This seems an unnecessary conclusion. On the basis of evidence of usage and experimental tests, one can try to formulate a systematic theoretical account of the system of concepts that an individual has attained and puts to use, and further, to elaborate the a priori system of principles, conditions, and assumptions that led him to construct this system from his limited experience. It is difficult to see why such an enterprise, whatever its chances of success, reflects a "Protean metaphysical urge." It seems a fully intelligible program. Any theory of attained concepts or of the basis for the acquisition of a system of concepts will, to be sure, be underdetermined by evidence—the task is not a triviality. Furthermore, there is no antecedent reason to suppose that induction or "generalization," in any clear sense

[17] David Pears, "Universals," in Antony Flew, ed., *Logic and Language*, Second Series (New York: Philosophical Library, 1953), pp. 63, 64.

of these notions, will have much to do with the matter.

Russell assumes, with Wittgenstein and many others, that there are "two ways of getting to know what a word means": verbal definition, in terms of other words, or direct ostensive definition.[18] As a description of fact, this is dubious. True verbal definition is probably a very rare event. The difficulty of giving a verbal definition of ordinary concepts is well known. Consider the attempts, still surely only partially successful, to define such concepts as "game" or "promise," for example. What we generally call "verbal definitions" are mere hints, that can be interpreted properly by someone who already controls a rich, highly articulated theory of language and the world. But surely the same is true of "ostensive definition." Again, neither Mill's canons nor any other known scheme will account for the uniformity and specificity with which a child or an adult will understand what a new word means or denotes, under the conditions of ostensive definition. This will become quite obvious to anyone who attempts, say, to program a computer to do likewise. Under normal conditions we learn words by a limited exposure to their use. Somehow, our brief and personal and limited contacts with the world suffice for us to determine what words mean. When we try to analyze any specific instance—say, such readily learned words as "mistake," or "try," or "expect," or "compare," or "die," or even common nouns—we find that rather rich assumptions about the world of fact and the interconnections of concepts come into play in placing the item properly in the system of language. This is by now a familiar observation, and I need not elaborate

[18] *Human Knowledge*, p. 18.

on it. But it seems to me to further dissipate the lingering
appeal of an approach to acquisition of knowledge that
takes empiricist assumptions as a point of departure for
what are presumed to be the simplest cases.

In fact, what substance is there to the claim that one
part of empiricist theory appears to be true without
any qualifications: namely, that words which I understand derive their meaning from my experience? That
experience is required to bring innate structures into
operation, to activate a system of innate ideas, is assumed quite explicitly, by Descartes, Leibniz, and others,
as an integral part of theories that can hardly be re-
garded as "empiricist" if the term is to retain any significance. Beyond this, such differences as exist among
individuals and across languages in the systems of concepts employed must be attributed to experience, if we
assume, as seems reasonable, that there is no specific
genetic adaptation to one or another language, and if we
abstract away from individual variation in mental capacity. How extensive are these differences? An empirical
question, obviously, but what little is known about the
specificity and complexity of belief as compared with
the poverty of experience leads one to suspect that it is
at best misleading to claim that words that I understand
derive their meaning from my experience.

Wittgenstein argued that "a word hasn't got a meaning given to it, as it were, by a power independent of us,
so that there could be a kind of scientific investigation
into what the word really means. A word has the meaning someone has given to it."[19] If the reference is to

---

[19] Ludwig Wittgenstein, *Blue and Brown Books* (Harper &
Row, Harper Torchbooks, 1958), p. 28.

conscious, explicit explanations of meanings (or the readiness to give them, as Wittgenstein sometimes implies), the assertion can hardly be accepted. On the other hand, we can easily imagine how an organism initially endowed with conditions on the form and organization of language could construct a specific system of interconnections among concepts, and conditions of use and reference, on the basis of scanty evidence. There is no inherent mystery in this. For such an organism, we could certainly carry out a scientific investigation of these systematic structures and conditions, and it is unclear why this should not be described as part of a scientific investigation of what words really mean. Words would have the meaning given to them by the organism, to be sure, though there would be no necessity to suppose that this "giving of meaning" is conscious or accessible to introspection, or that the organism is at all capable of explaining the system of concepts it uses or describing the characteristics of particular items with any accuracy. In the case of humans, there is every reason to suppose that the semantic system of language is given largely by a power independent of conscious choice; the operative principles of mental organization are presumably inaccessible to introspection, but there is no reason why they should in principle be more immune to investigation than the principles that determine the physical arrangement of limbs and organs.

In trying to develop a "behavioral" analysis of linguistic expressions and their meanings, Russell considers the environmental causes of uttering an expression, the effects of hearing it, and the effects which the

speaker expects or intends it to have on the hearer.[20]
The latter consideration leads us to an investigation of
reasons, as distinct from causes, and into the domain
of "mental acts." I will not consider whether the analysis Russell presents is very convincing (I do not believe
that it is), but here too he insists, quite correctly, that
a study of stimuli and responses, or habit structures, will
not get us very far. Though consideration of intended
effects avoids some problems, it seems to me that no
matter how fully elaborated, it will at best provide an
analysis of successful communication, but not of meaning or of the use of language, which need not involve
communication or even the attempt to communicate. If
I use language to express or clarify my thoughts, with
the intent to deceive, to avoid an embarrassing silence,
or in a dozen other ways, my words have a strict meaning and I can very well mean what I say, but the fullest
understanding of what I intend my audience (if any) to
believe or to do might give little or no indication of the
meaning of my discourse.

Russell suggests that the existence of "natural kinds"
—a tendency for properties to cluster in limited varieties
in the empirical world—facilitates common-sense inference, and that scientific knowledge is grounded in a
series of principles that he develops in an interesting and
detailed analysis. As an example, consider this principle:

> The physical world consists of units of a small
> number of different kinds, and there are causal
> laws governing the simpler structures that can be

[20] Bertrand Russell, *An Inquiry into Meaning and Truth*
(London: George Allen & Unwin, 1940), p. 27 and elsewhere.

built out of such units, causing such structures to
fall into a rather small number of discretely differ-
ing kinds. There are also complexes of events
which act as causal units, being preceded and followed throughout some finite time by a series of
complexes of events all having approximately the
same structure and interrelated by spatiotemporal
contiguity.

The physical world, Russell writes, "has what might be
called 'habits', i.e., causal laws; the behaviour of animals has habits, partly innate, partly acquired," gen-
erated by "animal inference." "Owing to the world
being such as it is, certain kinds of inductions are justi-
fied and others are not." By reflection on such processes,
we arrive at canons of inference which "are valid if the
world has certain characteristics which we all believe it
to have."[21]

We might say, paraphrasing these remarks, that our
mental constitution permits us to arrive at knowledge
of the world insofar as our innate capacity to create
theories happens to match some aspect of the structure
of the world. By exploring various faculties of the mind,
we might, in principle, come to understand what theories
are more readily accessible to us than others, or what
potential theories are accessible to us at all, what forms
of scientific knowledge can be attained, if the world is
kind enough to have the required properties. Where
it is not, we may be able to develop a kind of "intellectual technology"—say, a technique of prediction that
will, for some reason, work within limits—but not to
attain what might properly be called scientific under-

[21] Russell, *Human Knowledge*, pp. 495–96.

standing or common-sense knowledge. Another organism, following different principles, might develop other sciences, or lack some of ours. Whether we will come to understand those aspects of human existence or physical reality, features of which intrigue us, we do not know, though the question might be answerable if we were to succeed in determining the principles of human understanding. It is this task that Russell's mature theory of knowledge presents to us, in an outline that is suggestive but, as he insists, no more than that.

To pursue this task, we must investigate specific domains of human knowledge or systems of belief, determine their character, and study their relation to the brief and personal experience on which they are erected. A system of knowledge and belief results from the interplay of innate mechanisms, genetically determined maturational processes, and interaction with the social and physical environment. The problem is to account for the system constructed by the mind in the course of this interaction. The particular system of human knowledge that has, so far, lent itself most readily to such an approach is the system of human language. In the study of language we need not (to a first approximation, at least) make the distinction between knowledge and belief. There is no objective external standard against which to check the system of rules and principles relating sound and meaning—the grammar—constructed by the mind. By definition, a person knows his language (or several dialects and languages) perfectly, though we can ask how the system created by one speaker matches that of another. It seems to make little sense to say that a mature speaker does not know his own dialect, say, of English; though it might be that there are idiosyncratic features that distinguish his grammar from that of the speech communities in which he lives. At least, this is true to the extent—not inconsiderable—that we can divorce the study of language and its structure from questions of empirical belief and knowledge of fact. In one sense, a person's knowledge of language reflects his capacity to acquire knowledge in a relatively "pure form." One might argue, for this reason, that this is not a "central case" of human knowledge, and perhaps not an illuminating case.[22] It seems to me that caution is in order. We can raise seriously the question of acquisition of knowledge only where we have a reasonably convincing characterization of what has been learned. We lack any such characterization in the case of standard examples of common-sense knowledge or belief: for example, with regard to the behavior of physical objects, or human social behavior, or the relations of action and motives, and so on.

Some have argued rather differently, proposing that acquisition of language is based on more general principles that underlie other forms of learning as well. Such views will gain substance to the extent that their proponents can show how specific aspects of knowledge of language—some of which I will discuss in a moment —can be explained in terms of more general "learning strategies" or "principles of development." Since only the vaguest of suggestions have been offered, it is impossible, at present, to evaluate these proposals.

[22] See Roy Edgely, "Innate Ideas," in G. N. A. Vesey, ed., *Knowledge and Necessity*, Royal Institute of Philosophy Lectures (New York: St. Martin's Press, 1970), for an interesting discussion of this matter.

Knowledge of language results from the interplay of initially given structures of mind, maturational processes, and interaction with the environment. Thus there is no reason to expect that there will be invariant properties of the knowledge that is acquired—the grammars constructed by the mind—even if the innate determination of initial structures and maturational processes is quite restrictive. Suppose, however, that we discover certain invariant properties of human language. In such a case it is always a plausible (though not necessarily correct) hypothesis that these invariants reflect properties of mind, just as, if we were to discover invariant properties of the song of some species of bird, it would be plausible to suggest that these are genetically determined. This is an empirical hypothesis, falsifiable by factual evidence. The alternative to it would be the hypothesis that the invariants in question result from certain well-defined "learning strategies" applied to a sufficiently uniform environment. In the cases I will discuss, and many others, this alternative seems to me most implausible. In any case, the empirical conditions of the investigation are clear.

Invariance can appear at several levels of abstraction and significance. For example, in investigating a particular dialect of English, we discover similarities of usage among speakers of varying personal experience. Furthermore, investigation of a wide range of languages reveals invariant properties that are by no means necessary for a system of thought and communication. For example, it is conceivable that the principle of "nameability" in some language might be the simple condition that Russell investigates: that a continuous portion of space-time is a possible "nameable thing." But in human languages, it seems that other conditions enter into determining what are "nameable" things, as noted earlier. As we investigate other aspects of the representation of meaning, additional properties of language come to light. Consider the meaning of sentences. Some aspects of sentence meaning are determined by the ordering of words and their arrangement into phrases, while others are related to structures of a much more abstract sort. To take a simple case, consider the sentences "John appealed to Bill to like himself" and "John appeared to Bill to like himself."[23] The two sentences are virtually identical in surface form, but obviously quite different in interpretation. Thus when I say "John appealed to Bill to like himself," I mean that Bill is to like himself; but when I say "John appeared to Bill to like himself," it is John who likes himself. It is only at what I would call the level of "deep structure" that the semantically significant grammatical relations are directly expressed in this case.

The example illustrates relations of meaning among words, but semantic representation involves relations among phrases as well. Suppose I say, "I would speak about such matters with enthusiasm." The statement is ambiguous: it may mean that my speaking would be enthusiastic, or that I would be pleased to speak about such matters. The phrase "with enthusiasm" is associated either with the verb "speak" or with the phrase "speak about such matters." Investigating questions of

[23] The example is due to R. Dougherty. In subsequent discussion, I will borrow freely, without further specific attribution, from the work of Joan Bresnan, Howard Lasnik, Michael Helke, Paul Postal, and others.

this nature, we can, I believe, develop some reasonable though still only partial and tentative hypotheses as to how the meaning of sentences must be represented in human language, and how such representations relate to various aspects of linguistic form: order, phrasing, and abstract structures that relate in no simple way to the physical utterance.

Turning to the physical aspect of language, we reach similar conclusions. There are many imaginable physical dimensions that might, in principle, be used to determine the sounds of speech, but in fact the variety of human languages makes use of only a restricted range of properties. Furthermore, as the study of language has revealed since Ferdinand de Saussure's pioneering work, the sounds of language enter into systematic relations in accordance with restrictive principles. More remarkable still is the fact that the systematic structure of sound patterns is revealed most strikingly when we consider, not the sounds themselves in their physical aspect, but rather an abstract sound pattern that is mapped into a physical representation by ordered rules of a narrowly constrained type, rules which, applying in sequence, convert an abstract underlying representation of sound into a physical structure that may not bear a close point-by-point resemblance to the underlying mental representation. It is in this domain, in my opinion, that recent studies of language have obtained some of their most important insights.[24]

[24] See Noam Chomsky and Morris Halle, *Sound Patterns of English* (New York: Harper & Row, 1968), for a presentation of a general theory of sound structure applied to English. See also the more recent work of Steven Anderson, Michael Brame, Joan Bresnan, Charles Kisseberth, and others.

By studying the representation of sound and the representation of meaning in natural language, we can obtain some understanding of invariant properties that might reasonably be attributed to the organism itself as its contribution to the task of acquisition of knowledge, the schematism that it applies to the data of sense in its effort to organize experience and construct cognitive systems. But some of the most interesting and surprising results concern rather the system of rules that relate sound and meaning in natural language. These rules fall into various categories and exhibit invariant properties that are by no means necessary for a system of thought or communication, a fact that once again has intriguing implications for the study of human intelligence.

Consider, for example, the way in which questions are formed in English. Consider the sentence "The dog in the corner is hungry." From this, we can form the question "Is the dog in the corner hungry?" by a simple formal operation: moving the element "is" to the front of the sentence. Given a variety of examples of question formation, a linguist studying English might propose several possible rules of question formation. Imagine two such proposals. The first states that to form a question, we first identify the subject noun phrase of the sentence, and we then move the occurrence of "is" following this noun phrase to the beginning of the sentence. Thus in the example in question, the subject noun phrase is "the dog in the corner"; we form the question by moving the occurrence of "is" that follows it to the front of the sentence. Let us call this operation a "structure-dependent operation," meaning by this that the operation considers not merely the sequence of elements that constitute the sentence but also their structure; in this case, the fact that the sequence "the dog in the corner" is a phrase, furthermore a noun phrase. For the case in question, we might also have proposed a "structure-independent operation": namely, take the leftmost occurrence of "is" and move it to the front of the sentence. We can easily determine that the correct rule is the structure-dependent operation. Thus if we have the sentence "The dog that is in the corner is hungry," we do not apply the proposed structure-independent operation, forming the question "Is the dog that ———— in the corner is hungry?" Rather, we apply the structure-dependent operation, first locating the noun-phrase subject "the dog that is in the corner," then inverting the occurrence of "is" that follows it, forming: "Is the dog that is in the corner ———— hungry?"

Though the example is trivial, the result is nonetheless surprising, from a certain point of view. Notice that the structure-dependent operation has no advantages from the point of view of communicative efficiency or "simplicity." If we were, let us say, designing a language for formal manipulations by a computer, we would certainly prefer structure-independent operations. These are far simpler to carry out, since it is only necessary to scan the words of the sentence, paying no attention to the structures into which they enter, structures that are not marked physically in the sentence at all. Mathematicians have studied structure-independent operations on strings (inversion, shuffling, etc.), but it has occurred to no one to investigate the curious and complex notion of "structure-dependent operation," in the relevant sense. Notice further that we have very little evidence, in our normal experience, that the structure-dependent operation is the correct one. It is quite possible for a person to go through life without having heard any relevant examples that would choose between the two principles. It is, however, safe to predict that a child who has had no such evidence would unerringly apply the structure-dependent operation the first time he attempts to form the question corresponding to the assertion "The dog that is in the corner is hungry." Though children make certain kinds of errors in the course of language learning, I am sure that none make the error of forming the question "Is the dog that in the corner is hungry?" despite the slim evidence of experience and the simplicity of the structure-independent rule. Furthermore, all known formal operations in the grammar of English, or of any other language, are structure-dependent. This is a very simple example of an invariant principle of language, what might be called a formal linguistic universal or a principle of universal grammar.

Given such facts, it is natural to postulate that the idea of structure-dependent operations is part of the innate schematism applied by the mind to the data of experience. The idea is "innate to the mind" in the sense in which Descartes argued that "the idea of a true triangle" is innate: "because we already possess within us the idea of a true triangle, and it can be more easily conceived by our mind than the more complex figure of the triangle drawn on paper, we, therefore, when we see that composite figure, apprehend not it itself, but rather the authentic triangle."[25] As noted earlier, there

[25] *The Philosophical Works of Descartes,* trans. E. S. Haldane and G. R. T. Ross (New York: Dover Publications, 1955),

are now the glimmerings of understanding of the neuro-physiological structures that provide such schemata for interpretation of experience in the case of figures and objects, though the neurophysiology of language remains almost a total mystery. It does seem quite reasonable to propose, however, that the unknown structures of the brain that provide knowledge of language on the basis of the limited data available to us "possess within themselves" the idea of structure-dependent operations.

Studying language more carefully, we find many other examples of quite remarkable properties that appear to be inexplicable on the basis of experience alone. To take another simple case, consider the sentence "I believe the dog to be hungry." There is a corresponding passive: "The dog is believed to be hungry." We might propose, as a first approximation, that the passive is formed by the structure-dependent operation that locates the main verb and the noun phrase that follows it, inverting the two, and adding various modifications that need not concern us.

Consider next the sentence "I believe the dog's owner to be hungry." Applying the postulated operation, we locate the main verb "believe" and the noun phrase

---

Vol. 2, pp. 227–28. For further discussion and references, see my *Cartesian Linguistics* (New York: Harper & Row, 1966); *Aspects of the Theory of Syntax* (Cambridge, Mass.: The M.I.T. Press, 1965), Chap. 1; and *Language and Mind* (New York: Harcourt Brace Jovanovich, 1968). On English precursors of Kant in the study of the "conformity of objects to our mode of cognition" and "rationalistic idealism" more generally, see Arthur Lovejoy, "Kant and the English Platonists," *Essays Philosophical and Psychological: In Honor of William James* (New York: Longmans, Green & Company, 1908).

"the dog" following it, as before, and form "The dog is believed 's owner to be hungry." Obviously, this is incorrect. What we must do is choose not the noun phrase "the dog," but rather the noun phrase of which it is a part, "the dog's owner," giving then: "The dog's owner is believed to be hungry." The instruction for forming passives was ambiguous: the ambiguity is resolved by the overriding principle that we must apply the operation to the largest noun phrase that immediately follows the verb. This, again, is a rather general property of the formal operations of syntax. There has been some fairly intensive investigation of such conditions on formal operations in the past decade, and although we are far from a definitive formulation, some interesting things have been learned. It seems reasonably clear that these conditions must also be part of the schematism applied by the mind in language-learning. Again, the conditions seem to be invariant, insofar as they are understood at all, and there is little data available to the language-learner to show that they apply.

An interesting property of the formal operations of language is that though they are structure-dependent, they are, in an important sense, independent of meaning. Compare the sentences "I believed your testimony," "I believed your testimony to be false," and "I believed your testimony to have been given under duress." The corresponding passives are "Your testimony was believed," "Your testimony was believed to be false," and "Your testimony was believed to have been given under duress." In all cases, the passive is formed by the rule informally described a moment ago. The rule pays no attention to the grammatical and semantic relations of the main verb to the noun phrase that follows it. Thus in "I believed your testimony," the noun phrase is the grammatical object of "believe." In "I believed your testimony to be false," it bears no relation to "believe," and is the subject of "be false." In "I believed your testimony to have been given under duress," it bears no relation to "believe" and is the grammatical object of the embedded verb "give." Yet in all cases, the rule applies blindly, caring nothing for these differences.[26] Thus in an important sense, the rules are structure-dependent and only structure-dependent. Technically, they are rules that apply to abstract labeled bracketing of sentences (abstract, in that it is not physically indicated), not to systems of grammatical or semantic relations. Again, there is no a priori necessity for this to be true. These characteristics of language, if true, are empirical facts. It is reasonable to suppose that they are "a priori" for the organism, in that they define, for him, what counts as a human language, and determine the general character of his acquired knowledge of language. But it is easy to imagine systems of language that would depart from these principles. If our hypotheses are cor-

---

[26] It might be argued that the latter two sentences derive, not by passivization, but by "*it*-replacement" from "it is believed [your testimony . . .]." If so, the same comments apply to this rule and the others involved in the derivation. It should be noted that lexical properties of particular items determine the permissibility of transformations and that rules of semantic interpretation may be inapplicable in certain cases if transformations have applied. This "filtering effect" of transformations in effect makes them inapplicable in certain cases.

rect, such systems should be impossible for human children to learn in the normal way, though perhaps they might be learned as a kind of puzzle or intellectual exercise.

I might mention at this point that this account is extremely misleading in that I have spoken of formal operations on sentences. In fact, the careful study of language shows that these operations apply to abstract forms underlying sentences, to structures that may be quite remote from the actual physical events that constitute spoken or written language. (As noted earlier, the same is true in the case of sound structure.) These structures and the operations that apply to them are postulated as mental entities in our effort to understand what one has learned, when he has come to know a human language, and to explain how sentences are formed and understood. I would like to emphasize that there is nothing strange or occult in this move, any more than in the postulation of genes or electrons. For simplicity of exposition, I will continue to use the misleading notion of "operations on sentences," but the oversimplification should be borne in mind.

The account is misleading in another respect as well. The rules in question are not laws of nature, nor, of course, are they legislated or laid down by any authority. They are, if our theorizing is correct, rules that are constructed by the mind in the course of acquisition of knowledge. They can be violated, and in fact, departure from the rules can often be an effective literary device. To take a particularly simple example, Rebecca West, in criticism of the view that art reflects nature, wrote: "A copy of the universe is not what is required of art;

one of the damned thing is ample."[27] The statement violates the rule of grammar that requires a plural noun in such phrases as "one of the books is here" or "one of the damned things is enough." But the statement is nevertheless exactly to the point. We can often exploit the expressive resources of language most fully by departing from its principles. The "degree of logical or grammatical disorder" is one of William Empson's dimensions of ambiguity: deviation from strict grammatical rule is one device to force the reader to "invent a variety of reasons and order them in his own mind" in seeking to determine the meaning of what is said— "the essential fact about the poetical use of language," Empson suggests, but a feature of normal usage as well, for similar reasons.[28] This too should be borne in mind when I speak loosely about what can and cannot be said, grammatically.

The examples I have mentioned so far have been discussed in recent literature.[29] To illustrate further, I would like to turn to some still unexplored territory. I mentioned a moment ago that we form passives by inverting the main verb of a sentence and the noun phrase that follows it. Sometimes, however, the opera-

[27] Cited by M. H. Abrams in *The Mirror and the Lamp: Romantic Theory and the Critical Tradition* (New York: Oxford University Press, 1953) , p. 100.

[28] William Empson, *Seven Types of Ambiguity* (New York: New Directions Pub. Corp., 1947) , pp. 48. 25.

[29] For a more careful discussion of the topics that follow and related questions, see my "Conditions on Transformations," to appear in Steven Anderson and R. P. V. Kiparsky, eds., *Studies Presented to Morris Halle* (New York: Holt, Rinehart & Winston, forthcoming) .

tion is impermissible. Consider the sentence "I believe the dog is hungry." We cannot form "The dog is believed is hungry," though from the sentence "I believe the dog to be hungry" we can form "The dog is believed to be hungry." How can we account for this difference? It might, of course, be that this is simply an idiosyncrasy of English, learned by experience. Let us explore the more interesting possibility that this is not so, and ask what kinds of principles might account for such a difference.

To begin with, notice that the two sentences in question ("I believe the dog is hungry," "I believe the dog to be hungry") consist of the subject "I," the main verb "believe," and an embedded structure of the form of a sentence: "the dog is hungry," "the dog to be hungry." Let us distinguish two types of embedded sentences: tensed sentences such as "the dog is hungry" and nontensed sentences such as "the dog to be hungry." Only the former, of course, can appear as a nonembedded sentence. As a first guess, let us propose the principles that nothing can be extracted from a tensed sentence.

Other examples suggest that this principle can be generalized. Consider the sentence "The candidates each hated the other." A variant is "The candidates hated each other." There are persuasive arguments, which I will not review here, that the latter is formed from the former by a rule that moves the word "each" over the main verb, replacing the word "the" of the object phrase "the other." Consider next the sentence "The candidates each expected the other to win." Applying the rule, we can form "The candidates expected each other to win."

ider next the sentence "The candidates each expected that the other would win" or "The candidates each believed the other would win." We cannot apply the rule, in either case, to form "The candidates expected that each other would win" or "The candidates believed each other would win." To account for this difference, let us generalize our earlier principle and propose that nothing can be extracted from or introduced into an embedded tensed sentence. More generally, let us propose that no rule can involve the phrase X and the phrase Y, where Y is contained in a tensed sentence to the right of X: i.e., no rule can involve X and Y in the structure $[\ldots X \ldots [\ldots Y \ldots] \ldots]$, where $[\ldots Y \ldots]$ is a tensed sentence.

Before investigating some apparent counterexamples to this principle, let us consider some cases that suggest still another condition relating embedded structures and phrases outside them. Consider the sentence "John expected to win." It has generally been assumed, in modern studies of English grammar, that this derives from an underlying structure containing an embedded sentence of the form: noun phrase—win, where a rule assigns an anaphoric relation, a relation of coreference in this case, to the noun phrase and the subject of the full sentence. The embedded noun phrase is then deleted. Thus if grammatical relations are assigned prior to deletion, it will follow that "John" will be understood to be the subject of "win" as well as of "expect" in "John expected to win," as is of course the case. There are syntactic reasons for this assumption, which I will not review. Let us accept it, then, taking the noun phrase of the embedded sentence to be a pronoun which is deleted after being assigned an anaphoric relation to its antecedent.

Consider next the sentence "The candidates each expected to defeat the other." By our assumption, this derives from the underlying form "The candidates each expected [pronoun—to defeat the other]," where brackets enclose the embedded nontensed sentence. By the rule of *each*-movement, followed by deletion of the pronoun, we derive "The candidates expected to defeat each other," in conformity with the facts.

Consider next the sentence "The men each expected the soldier to shoot the other." The rule of *each*-movement should apply, as in the preceding case, giving "The men expected the soldier to shoot each other." Obviously, this is incorrect. Some condition prevents movement of "each" into the embedded nontensed sentence in this case.

The principle that suggests itself at once is this: Where the embedded sentence contains a full subject, no rule can involve an item X to the left of this sentence and an item Y in its predicate. More formally, no rule can involve X and Y in the structure: ... X ... [Z — ... Y ...], where Z is the lexically specified subject of ... Y .... Loosely put, no rule can relate items across the subject of an embedded phrase. This principle is supported by many other examples. Consider the sentence "The candidates each heard denunciations of the other." The grammatical object of "heard" is the complex noun phrase "denunciations of the other." The principle of *each*-movement applies, giving "The candidates heard denunciations of each other." But suppose that this complex noun phrase contains a subject, as in "The candidates each heard John's denunciations of the other," where "John" is the subject of "denunciation."[30] We cannot, in this case, apply *each*-movement to give "The candidates heard John's denunciations of each other." The latter, though of course intelligible, is jarring to the ear in a way in which "The candidates heard denunciations of each other" is not. The suggested principle explains the distinction. Notice that in this case, the principle applies not to an embedded sentence but to an embedded complex noun phrase with the form of a sentence. The same distinction appears in the pair "The men saw pictures of each other," "The men saw John's pictures of each other." The same is true of many other cases.

These examples illustrate one case of the suggested principle: namely, that a general constraint blocks insertion of an item under the specified conditions. Similarly, extraction of an item is blocked under the same conditions. Consider the sentence "You saw pictures of someone." In colloquial English, we can form the corresponding question "Who did you see pictures of?" But the question "Who did you see John's pictures of?" from "You saw John's pictures of someone" is far less

---

[30] Use of the term "subject" requires explanation. For an appropriate definition and an explanation of why it is proper to regard "John" as the "subject" of "denounce," "denunciation," "picture," in "John denounced Bill," "John's denunciation of Bill," "John's picture of Bill," respectively, see my "Remarks on Nominalization," in R. A. Jacobs and P. S. Rosenbaum, eds., *Readings in English Transformational Grammar* (Boston: Ginn & Company, 1970). The careful reader will notice that I am using the term "subject of" with a slight ambiguity. Thus in "John denounces Bill," I refer to "John" as the subject of "denounces" and also as the subject of "denounces Bill." Similarly, in "John's denunciation of Bill."

natural, because of the cited principle. Again, there are similar cases with other constructions.

Consider a rule of a very different sort. It has been observed that such sentences as "I saw us" or "We saw me" are strange, as compared with "They saw us" or "I saw them." Suppose, then, that some rule of interpretation assigns the property "strangeness" to a sentence of the form: noun phrase—verb—noun phrase—X, where the two noun phrases intersect in reference. This is, no doubt, a special case of a more general principle of interpretation that leads us to try to assign difference of reference to noun phrases under a variety of formal conditions. Thus if I say "The soldiers detested the officers," you would naturally understand me as referring to a set of soldiers disjoint from the set of officers, though there is no semantic absurdity in considering the two sets to overlap—e.g., if the soldiers hated the officers among them, perhaps even themselves. In the case of the first-person pronouns, it is impossible to assign disjoint reference; hence the strangeness of the sentences.

But now consider the two sentences "I expected them to hate us" and "I expected us to hate them." Clearly the second, but not the first, has the property of strangeness of "I saw us." The principle in question explains the difference. The rule of interpretation does not apply, assigning strangeness, when the two personal pronouns "I" and "us" are separated by the subject of the embedded sentence.

Finally, let us turn to a somewhat more complex example. Consider the sentence "I didn't see many of the pictures." In colloquial usage, this would normally be interpreted as meaning "I saw few of the pictures," i.e., not many of the pictures are such that I saw them. There is a secondary interpretation, namely: Many of the pictures are such that I didn't see them. Under the latter interpretation, I could truly say "I didn't see many of the pictures" if there were a hundred pictures and I had seen just fifty. Thus I didn't see fifty, but I did see fifty others. Under the former and, I believe, more normal interpretation, I could not truly say "I didn't see many of the pictures" under these conditions, though I could truly say it if I had seen just three of the hundred pictures.

Consider next the sentence "I didn't see pictures of many of the children." Again, there are two interpretations. Under what I am calling the "normal" interpretation, it means that I saw pictures of few of the children. Under the secondary interpretation, it means "Pictures of many of the children are such that I didn't see them" (although perhaps I did see pictures of many of the children as well).

The "normal" interpretation in both cases associates "not" with "many." The secondary interpretation associates "not" with the main verb "see."

Consider next the sentence "I didn't see John's pictures of many of the children." Here, I believe, the "normal" interpretation is ruled out. The sentence cannot, without extreme artificiality, be interpreted as meaning "I saw John's pictures of (only) few of the children." For speakers who find the secondary interpretation unacceptable in the earlier cases, there will be no natural interpretation of this sentence. Other speakers, I believe, will interpret it naturally as meaning only

"John's pictures of many of the children are such that I didn't see them" (though perhaps I did see John's pictures of many of the children). Though the examples are moderately subtle, I think that this statement of the facts is correct. If so, notice that it follows from the principle in question. Association of "not" with "many" is ...ked by the principle that items cannot be related when separated by the subject of an embedded sentence.

Notice some interesting properties of the principles in question. First, they are extremely general, applying to formal operations that modify the form of sentences as well as rules of interpretation of sentences. Second, they appear to have no obvious motivation on the basis of semantic or other considerations of communicative utility. Correspondingly, violation of the principles often gives intelligible though somewhat odd-sounding forms. These characteristics are typical of many of the general conditions that have been tentatively proposed as linguistic universals, formal invariants of language.

Let us turn briefly to some apparent violations of the principles. Consider the sentence "Did you tell me that Bill was there?" Correspondingly, we can form the question "Where did you tell me that Bill was?" This operation violates both of the conditions I have proposed. The question-word "where" is extracted from the embedded tensed sentence "Bill was there" and furthermore, it is moved over the subject of this sentence. How can we account for these violations, for the difference between this operation and the others that we have discussed?

There is strong evidence that the underlying form of sentences consists not merely of a subject and a predicate, but of the structure: complementizer—subject—predicate, where the complementizer can be null in the output, but can also be realized as such items as "that," "for," and question-words, as in *"That the dog was hungry* surprised me," *"For the dog to be hungry* is odd," *"What the dog ate* is unknown," and so on. Let us propose that to form questions, the question-words move into the complementizer position. Let us now modify our principles to permit an item to escape from a tensed sentence if and only if it is in the complementizer position. I will also invoke here another well-confirmed principle, namely, that operations apply in a cyclic fashion, first to the most deeply embedded structures, then to the structures that contain them, and so on.

Consider now our problem sentence "Where did you tell me that Bill was?" The underlying structure is: complementizer—you tell me [complementizer—Bill—was somewhere]. In the first cycle, we form "where" from "somewhere" and move the question-word to the embedded complementizer position, violating no principles. This yields: complementizer—you tell me [where Bill was]. In the second cycle, we reapply the rule, moving "where" to the complementizer position of the main sentence, as is now permitted by the modification of the principles. This gives "Where did you tell me (that) Bill was?"[31] Depending on semantic properties of the main verb, the rule may or may not apply on the second cycle. If it does not, we derive such sentences as "I wonder where Bill was."

These proposals have several empirical conse-

[31] I omit here some technical details, e.g., the rules that spell out the complementizer position optionally as "that."

quences. I will not trace the reasoning in detail, but the reader can determine for himself that they block such sentences as "Where do you wonder whom Bill saw?" from the abstract form "You wonder [Bill saw someone somewhere.]" The same considerations block "Whom do you wonder whether Bill saw" or "What does Bill know how we do?" though they will permit "Whom do you think (that) Bill saw?" or "What does Bill know how to do?" for example. These principles predict that an item will be able to escape from an embedded sentence in apparent violation of the principles just in case there is, on independent grounds, a rule that moves the item to the complementizer po⌐ ⌐on of the sentence. Thus question-words can escape   ⌐ne is impossible from the complex noun phrase "John's picture of Bill," since noun phrases contain no complementizer (thus "Whom did you see John's picture of?" is blocked). Similarly, escape is impossible in the case of passivization applied to "I believe John was here" (blocking "John is believed is here"), since there is no independent rule moving the subject of the embedded sentence to the complementizer position.

Space limits prevent further discussion, but it is not difficult to show that if these principles are carefully formulated, they will also account for many other well-known distinctions: for example, the distinction between "Whom do you believe that John saw?" (from "You believe that John saw someone") and the impossible "Whom do you believe the claim that John saw?" (from "You believe the claim that John saw someone"). The result follows from careful definition of the principle of cyclic application: the rule forming questions applies to adjacent structures, that is, one structure and another in which the first is directly embedded. A number of other interesting consequences follow, if we pursue the matter further.

The major point that I want to show, by this brief and informal discussion, is that there apparently are deep-seated and rather abstract principles of a very general nature that determine the form and interpretation of entences. It is reasonable to formulate the empirical ypothesis that such principles are language universals. Quite probably the hypothesis will have to be qualified as research into the variety of languages continues. To the extent that such hypotheses are tenable, it is plausible to attribute the proposed language invariants to the innate language faculty which is, in turn, one component of the structure of mind. These are, I stress, empirical hypotheses. Alternatives are conceivable. For example, one might argue that children are sp :ifically trained to follow the principles in question, or, more plausibly, that these principles are special cases of more general principles of mind. As already noted, it is impossible to evaluate such suggestions until they are given some reasonable formulation.

I have stressed throughout that in the cases discussed there appears to be no general explanation for the observed phenomena in terms of communicative efficiency or "simplicity." In other words, there seems to be no "functional explanation" for the observations in question. In some cases the principles may serve to reduce ambiguity, but at most marginally. One can easily imagine systems of communication or expression of thought that have structure-independent operations,

operations on networks of semantic relations, operations that violate the formal principles suggested, or conditions that would eliminate the possibility of such ambiguities as we find commonly in natural language (e.g., consider "She is too old-fashioned to marry," where "she" may be interpreted as subject or object of "marry"; it is easy to imagine conditions that would eliminate such ambiguities, but they do not operate, so far as is known, in natural languages). There is no particular reason, so far as I can see, why a language used for the purposes of natural language could not depart from the formal principles discussed and proposed here. This fact, if fact it is, is important. A traditional view holds that language is "a mirror of mind." This is true, in some interesting sense, insofar as properties of language are "species-specific"—not explicable on some general grounds of functional utility or simplicity that would apply to arbitrary systems that serve the purposes of language. Where properties of language can be explained on such "functional" grounds, they provide no revealing insight into the nature of mind. Precisely because the explanations proposed here are "formal explanations," precisely because the proposed principles are not essential or even natural properties of any imaginable language, they provide a revealing mirror of mind (if correct). Such principles, we may speculate, are a priori for the species—they provide the framework for the interpretation of experience and the construction of specific forms of knowledge on the basis of experience—but are not necessary or even natural properties of all imaginable systems that might serve the functions of human language. It is for this reason that these principles